To the You Who Used to Be

To the You Who Used to Be

Poems on Dementia and Wholeness

Patricia McKernon Runkle

SHANTI ARTS PUBLISHING

BRUNSWICK, MAINE

To the You Who Used to Be
Poems on Dementia and Wholeness

Published by Shanti Arts Publishing

Designed by Shanti Arts Designs

Cover image is a photograph of Frances Perry McKernon
taken in 1941 and provided by the author.

Shanti Arts LLC
193 Hillside Road
Brunswick, Maine 04011
shantiarts.com

Printed in the United States of America

ISBN: 978-1-962082-55-6 (softcover)

Library of Congress Control Number (LCCN): 2024948695

for my mother,
Frances Perry McKernon

Contents

Acknowledgments

The author extends her gratitude to the editors of the following publications in which these poems first appeared:

The Final Lilt of Songs: A Poetry Anthology (South Mountain-Watchung Poets, 2008): "Venus in the Morning"

Frogpond: "Walking to the Funeral" (Vol. 34.1, Winter 2011)

Full of Moonlight: Haiku Society of America 2016 Members' Anthology: "Acorn"

Grey Sparrow: "Alz" (Issue 11, Winter 2012)

Journal of New Jersey Poets: "Given the Mother Word *Pure*" (Issue 51, 2014); "Coin of the Realm" (Issue 55, 2018)

Modern Haiku: "Crocus" (Vol. 41.2, Summer 2010); "Back of the Cemetery Map"; "Lifting a Spoon"; and "A Swallow Glides" (Vol. 48.1, Winter-Spring 2017)

A Moment's Longing: Haiku Society of America Members' Anthology 2019: "Distant Phone Call"

The Stillwater Review: "Mid-May and the Daffs" and "Old Rose" (Vol. 13, Spring 2023)

The Temple Bell Stops: Contemporary Poems of Grief, Loss, and Change (Modern English Tanka Press, 2012): "Walking to the Funeral"

Visiting the Wind: Haiku Society of America Members' Anthology 2021: "Her Absence"

The Mother Word

Given the Mother Word *Pure*

There is a word I want
for something missing that isn't lost—
   not *mislaid* (slippers on a shelf)
   not *hidden* (trinkets in pockets)
   not *absent* (the way to your room).

We were sitting at a table in the day room
playing with Scrabble pieces,
making little words from big words.
   In *picture*, you saw *pure*.
   Then I scrambled *pure* to form
   a word you learned long ago.

From the burnt-out forest of your brain,
a memory leapt out.
  "Puer," you said, "that's—a boy."
   In that moment, you were all girl,
   fourteen, first-year Latin swinging
   branch to branch.

Where is the word I want
for something missing that isn't lost—
   unseen, yet flawlessly present.

A Parabolic Path

Venus in the Morning

Pale light in the window,
I want to gaze

at the beautiful planet
rowing across the sky

and muse on
my mother's quilt,

a patchwork
of family photos.

A black and white snapshot
shows her in a canoe

holding an oar, her head
tilted pertly to one side.

She is on her honeymoon.
Her sunny smile is for

the man behind the camera:
her love, her lover.

None of us is born.
None of us has died.

In 1941, she has the rippling lake,
the gently rocking boat,

and the hale young man
to whom she opens herself.

Her future is liquid,
light as a paddle.

Coin of
the Realm

He wouldn't
mind, he

said, who
won the

toss. Both
girls were

beautiful. Up
went a

nickel, down
came my

mother. Did
she land

on the
floor, hard?

Or softly,
in his

palm? Was
it only

his whimsy
at play?

This story
his way

of warning
the children

they might
not have

existed. That
arrival on

this globe
takes a

parabolic path.
That choices—

true false,
blind illumined—

all pay
their way,

a flip
and a

spin, to
shiver at

the door
of a

womb, on
the rim

of a
world.

crocus

I too began

in darkness

My First Mountain

When I saw the Rockies
for the first time, I thought
Mama, you should be here.

You let me sail
on the lake
at your foothills.

You let me scale you,
trail you, feast
at your peaks.

You let me see how high
the sky is, how heaven
and earth consort.

Old Rose

Old Rose would come tottering to our door,
crusty as a Roman coin dredged up from fathoms.
Benvenuta! my mother would say, and I'd scamper
to get the tea kettle going and fig bars out.

Rose would plant herself at the kitchen table,
smooth her black dress and release the fragrance
of Italian, my mother's mother's mother tongue
she hadn't heard since childhood.

So she'd ride waves of feeling, my mother—beam
when Rose smiled, shake her head when Rose frowned,
pat her hand when she got teary, all the while
teaching me

feel me feeling, know me knowing
words are boats bobbing

remember this
when I come to you disguised
as an old woman

Eighty-Seven

In the hubbub, I hear it

above clattering dishes
clinking glasses
the *tink-tink* of forks

quieter than the *tuk-tuk*
of your cane
softer than your in-breath
lighter than the wish
upon your candles

here, at the height
of the heart's register,
your children
let go of failures
disband factions
practice the art of ensemble
all, all for

your gladness,
the merry notes
that pipe us home.

The Long Silence

acorn

the long silence

of falling

distant phone call

in our pauses

each other's crickets

Alz

Being
        together
  now   is
      like
talking
  in   a
soundproof
            room...
    each
missing
            report
    buried
in   the

  silencing

      walls.

Ninety-Two

Not her memory but ours
gathers us today.

Your name, again?

One match lights every candle.
Tip kisses tip, and the moment blazes

Here goes nothin'!

only to be extinguished
in smoke and charred twine.

Your name, again?

One year, we all forgot her birthday.
Days later, I found her weeping,
folding laundry she had washed,
dried, hauled.
There was no retrieving
that lost day.

You're my children?

Each breath enters a different body,
each thought, a different mind.

Your name, again?

Where She Is, I Could Be

In the elevator
       my reflection fuzzy on the metal door
the only choices are levels E and G
       I must want E for East Wing
       where she is
I push E
       fabulously smooth ride
The doors open, I walk the hall
       23, 26?
More light in the hallway than I remember
       maybe it was cloudy last time
She's not here, though I peek in every room
       they moved her where?
I ask a nurse, who gazes at me just
   a moment too long, long enough to feel like
       being searched
I'll show you how to find her, she says
This is the entry level, you have to choose
    level G for ground
       but . . . but
I push G
       so jiggly this time
and adjust my badge. On the flip side,
    a code number that will release me at visit's end
now, a long walk through a gray corridor
    toward someone whose mind is muddled
       not clear like mine

autumn dusk

how long till my children

make my decisions?

Sprocket

Soon I'll be gone and so will her recollection of our visit

Nothing to hang it on, hold it, something's missing

I walk the corridor toward the locked and coded exit

past doors and posted snapshots

My steps inch me forward, my mind grips a word

sprocket, the cogged wheel that engages film

Each tooth fits a hole clipped out of the story

and holds, for a moment

a moment

lifting a spoon

to her lips

crickets in twilight

Communion

She holds the offering wrapped in foil
and a slip-cover case. Doesn't turn it over
to investigate, though she can read
the writing—*milk chocolate*. Just holds it.
The desire to taste cannot overcome
the problem of packaging.

I slip off the case, give back the gold-foiled disc
but her hands simply receive it.

So I peel one edge to reveal the scent. Her fingers
begin working but fumble, stop.

Four hands, twenty fingers later, the wafer is hers
and on her tongue. Together, we take in this moment.
It's good, she says, for both of us.

Then I wipe with a tissue the corners of her lips
as she so often ministered to me.

To the You Who Used to Be

The men on your ward will wear sweatpants and sweatshirts.
They won't shave themselves or talk to you.

So it will be an event when a clean-shaven man walks in wearing
a button-down shirt and dress pants. Smiles, speaks kind words.
The man is your son-in-law, but you won't know him
or recognize your daughter and granddaughters.

You're spending much of your time sleeping now.
The treasure of your language is reduced to one-
or two-bit expressions (*that's good, thank you, no*)
and those on a good day. Most days will not be good.

But there will be surprises. One day in summer
you'll see this son-in-law of yours and say
something never heard before or since—
Hello, Mr. Stylish—and astonish us.

We'll roll you through dim corridors, stale
and chilly air, out to the courtyard. A warm breeze
on your cheeks. Somewhere in the trees,
the voice of an oriole.

We'll look up—all in wordless wonder
at invisible loveliness.

A Song Like Incense

Mid-May and the Daffs

Mid-May and the daffs are past bloom,
    their chubby sunshine withered
        and twisted on the stem.

If she were my mother, I'd
    call in hospice now
        the head nurse says,
            but the doctor isn't ready
                to sign off. The young myrtle

we planted last fall
    has sprouted leaves on just half
        of its branches.
            And the first dandelions—

they've already run to seed.
    A cool breeze splits
        their airy crowns
            and ferries them
                in pieces
                    aloft.

a swallow glides

into the barn

my mother enters

hospice care

all souls' day

the stillness

of fallen leaves

walking to the funeral the long shadow ahead of me

her favorite aria

singing my sadness

home

A Song Like Incense

a pantoum for my mother,
a lifelong singer

a song

    like incense

        rides on air

        lofting

like incense

    in billowing notes

        lofting

        itself

in billowing notes

    a life singing

        itself

        a song

back of the cemetery map

blank in all directions

The Gravedigger's Spoon

In his brown work overalls
and denim jacket,
he enters our circle
with a long-handled spade
when prayers are concluded.

As a young man
he would come to our house
and eat my mother's spaghetti
the old-fashioned way,
topping his fork with a spoon.

Now he lifts
a decorative cloth
and a wooden plank
from the small hole he dug
for her remains.

When the urn is ensconced,
gently—for our sake, and because
he also once sat at her table—
he feeds, spoon by spoon,
the last open mouth.

her absence

arcing the night

new moon

a rosebush for my mother

from root to blossom

the long stem

Her Eyes Are Upturned

Her eyes are upturned to the camera
with vivacious curiosity.
Seated at a picnic table shaded by trees,
she is in the bloom of womanhood.
On her lap, her first child.

This photograph, like a telescope,
brings distant objects to mind
through a tunnel of years,
invites me to imagine
what's on the table outside
the frame—bowls of raspberries,
cherries, luscious fruits of summer.

The husk of her body now ash,
spring has just come.
In my garden is a risen daffodil shoot.
Its stem is tall, capped by a slender bud
that points to the sky. Wrapped inside,
the color of sun.

I tend it

it blossoms

gratitude

Gratitude for friends whose insights on these poems have helped to shape their final form, especially Marcia LeBeau, Judy Christian, Phil Kirsch, Heather Newman, Robin Rosen Chang, and Peggy Vassallo of South Mountain Poets; and members of Haiku Poets of the Garden State, present and past, too many to name here but every one of whom has deepened my understanding of this subtle art form.

Gratitude for Mary Ann, my sister and guiding light, who arranged for and coordinated the assisted living and nursing care our mother needed and made it possible for her to live with dignity in the last years of her life.

Gratitude for David, Anne, and Sarah, my husband and daughters, whose love is my foundation and my joy.

Gratitude for Frances, my mother, and Francis, my father, whose love I can never fully return and from whose lives I continue to learn.

About the Author

 Patricia McKernon Runkle's poems explore loss, healing, and the unexpected. Her memoir, *Grief's Compass: Walking the Wilderness with Emily Dickinson*, received a Nautilus Book Awards Silver Medal for lyrical prose and was a finalist for the Rubery Book Award. In addition to memoir and poetry, Patricia has written and published songs and collaborative choral pieces. She holds a master's degree in theological studies from Harvard Divinity School and values the quiet work of listening. She lives with her husband in New Jersey, and they cherish their two grown children.